Across North Carolina

Printed in Mexico

ISBN-13: 978-0-15-366972-9
ISBN-10: 0-15-366972-1

3 4 5 6 7 8 9 10   805   13 12 11 10 09 08

SCHOOL PUBLISHERS

Visit *The Learning Site!* www.harcourtschool.com

The Three Regions of North Carolina

Each of North Carolina's regions has something different to offer visitors and residents alike.

Three Regions, Endless Attractions

North Carolina is in the southeastern United States. From its Atlantic coast to its mountain ranges, North Carolina offers many options for any tourist.

The state has three regions, each with its own special features. These regions are the Coastal Plain in the east, the Piedmont in the middle, and the Mountains in the west.

The geographic features of each region shape the ways of life of the people who live there. Geography has affected the growth of major cities and of recreation areas. Farming communities and industries are also influenced by geography. Each region makes use of natural, human, and capital resources. Each region also has a history.

North Carolina also has several important universities. One of North Carolina's best-known colleges is the University of North Carolina at Chapel Hill. The first classes there were held in 1795. Duke University is well known for scientific research.

Tourist Attractions

Town Creek Indian Mound is popular among history buffs. This park preserves information about Native American life in centuries past.

Old Salem, with its Children's Museum and Toy Museum, lets visitors step back in time. The village presents life in North Carolina as it was from 1766 to 1840.

Sports fans also travel to the Piedmont. Golfers come for the beautiful golf courses. Fans of car racing can visit Lowe's Motor Speedway in Charlotte.

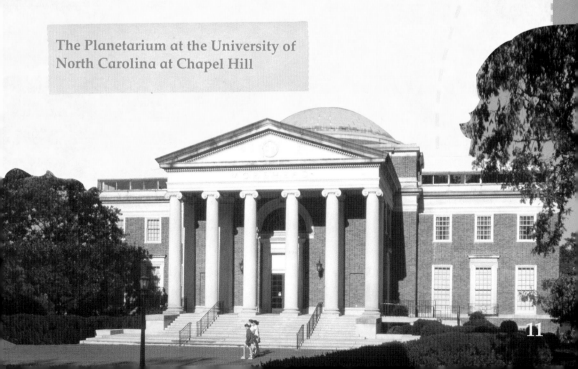

The Planetarium at the University of North Carolina at Chapel Hill

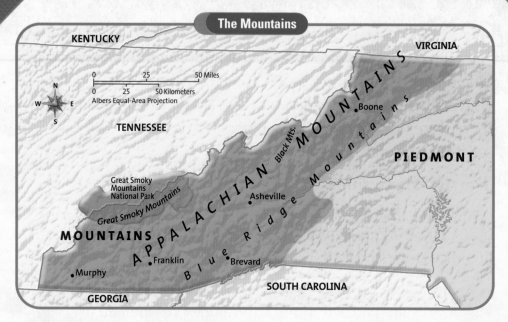

KENTUCKY

VIRGINIA

0   25   50 Miles
0   25   50 Kilometers
Albers Equal-Area Projection

TENNESSEE

Boone

Black Mts.

A P P A L A C H I A N   M O U N T A I N S

PIEDMONT

Great Smoky
Mountains
National Park

Great Smoky Mountains

Blue Ridge Mountains

Asheville

MOUNTAINS

Franklin

Brevard

Murphy

GEORGIA

SOUTH CAROLINA

The Great Smoky Mountains are a part of the
Mountains region.

Majestic Mountains

In the western part of the state, the Piedmont gives way
to the grand peaks of the Mountains region. The Blue Ridge
Mountains, the Black Mountains, and the Great Smoky
Mountains are the major ranges in the state. They form part
of the Appalachian Mountain chain, which stretches from
Alabama to Canada.

A National Treasure

Great Smoky Mountains National
Park is the nation's most-visited
national park. Each year, 10 million
people explore it. A smoke-like
mist wraps the mountains' peaks
and rests in the valleys.

Visitors flock to the mountains to admire the amazing views. They can enjoy many rivers, streams, and waterfalls. In the parks, people camp, hike, fish, and ride horses.

Visitors take pictures of white-tailed deer and black bears. Some drive along out-of-the-way roads. There, they see many original buildings from the past, including gristmills, barns, and schools.

A Place for All Seasons

Skiers and snowboarders like the mountains in winter, when they are covered with snow. In late spring and summer, visitors come to the cool mountains to beat the heat of the cities. Fall is also a beautiful time to visit the mountains. Trees at the highest elevations begin to put on their autumn colors in September.

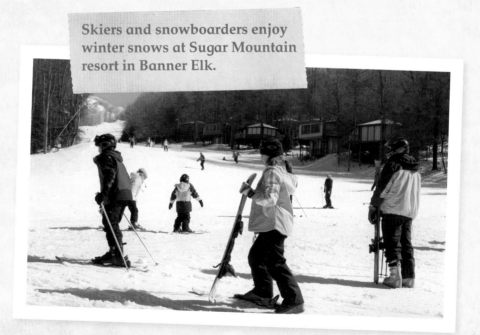

Skiers and snowboarders enjoy winter snows at Sugar Mountain resort in Banner Elk.

The Biltmore Estate

The Biltmore Estate is one of North Carolina's most popular places for visitors. A million people visit each year. The estate is on 8,000 acres of land in Asheville, the state's largest mountain city.

The house on the Biltmore Estate is the largest privately owned home in the United States. It has 250 rooms! The rooms hold many valuable antiques and works of art.

Outside, the grounds are made up of wild areas and formal gardens. A farm village, a winery, and a mill are on the property.

George Washington Vanderbilt

George Washington Vanderbilt built the Biltmore Estate. The Vanderbilts had developed a booming business shipping goods on ferries and railroads.

George W. Vanderbilt

When George Vanderbilt visited North Carolina's mountains, he loved what he saw. He bought 125,000 acres of land. Over time, he made plans to build a huge summer home there.

Vanderbilt was one of the nation's richest people. He poured money into the estate. Finally, in 1895, his summer home was completed.

Vanderbilt wanted his North Carolina home to support itself and the community. He also wanted it to be a fine home that he could enjoy with his friends. He built his estate to be a place where he could display the many treasures he had gathered from his travels. Today, the Biltmore is a national historic landmark.

North Carolina's diverse features offer visitors many interesting sights. It's no wonder people come from many places to travel across North Carolina.

A flower garden at the Biltmore Estate

Think and Respond

1. What are North Carolina's three regions?

2. What is the fall line?

3. How does North Carolina's land change from east to west?

4. Why do people settle in the Piedmont region?

5. Which of North Carolina's tourist destinations appeals to you the most? Why?

 # Activity

Use the library and school-approved websites to learn more about one of North Carolina's tourist attractions. Use what you learn to create a travel brochure. Share the brochure with your class.

A Popular Destination

North Carolina is a medium-sized state. It is the twenty-ninth state in size, yet it is the eleventh-largest in population. More than eight million people live in North Carolina.

North Carolina is a beautiful state that enjoys warm weather through much of the year. The geography and climate of the state make it a popular tourist destination. In fact, tourism has become an important industry in the state. About 200,000 people work in the tourism industry here.

Many people come to North Carolina for recreational activities and the beautiful scenery. They also come to learn about North Carolina's history. Whatever a person's interests, North Carolina has something to offer.

Hiking at Looking Glass Rock is a popular activity in North Carolina.

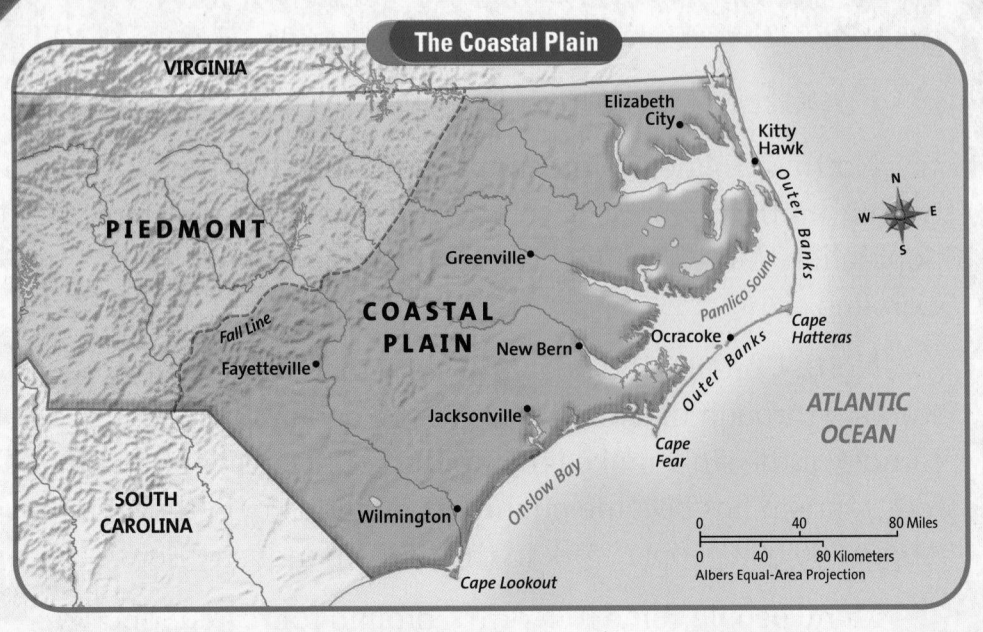

Some people think the Outer Banks look like the "boot" of Italy.

At the Ocean's Edge

North Carolina is the widest state east of the Mississippi River. Along the eastern shore is a chain of islands known as the Outer Banks. These sandy barrier islands protect North Carolina's shore. They keep it from wearing away.

On the Outer Banks are three capes that jut out into the Atlantic Ocean. These are Cape Fear, Cape Lookout, and Cape Hatteras. Wind and water have shaped the Outer Banks.

Kitty Hawk

Modern aviation began on the Outer Banks in 1903. The Wright brothers made their historic flight near Kitty Hawk, North Carolina. Today, tourists like to visit the Wright Brothers Memorial, where they can view a model of their plane, the Flyer.

Graveyard of the Atlantic

Strong winds whip across the Outer Banks. The Atlantic Ocean beats the shore so that the sands shift constantly. The actions of water and wind have made the Outer Banks a dangerous area for shipping.

The area around Cape Hatteras has a deadly nickname—"Graveyard of the Atlantic." The underwater sandbars off the coast have caused more than 1,000 shipwrecks over the years.

Cape Hatteras

Tourists and the Outer Banks

Tourists flock to North Carolina's Outer Banks for vacations. They come for the sunny weather, miles and miles of sandy beaches, and great fishing. Visitors can ride bicycles along the islands' many trails. At Cape Hatteras, they can climb 208 feet to the top of the tallest lighthouse in the United States.

Shipwrecks are found all along the Outer Banks.

From the Swamps to the Farmlands

West of the Outer Banks are low, wet marshlands. Many different kinds of plant and animal life can be found here. Ecotourists are drawn to these swampy lands. Ecotourists are visitors who enjoy wild places in a careful way that protects the wildlife.

The Great Dismal Swamp

North Carolina shares the Great Dismal Swamp with the state of Virginia. The swamp is a protected habitat. Black bears, bobcats, red foxes, and poisonous snakes live there. So do whitetail deer, spotted turtles, and salamanders. Black gum and cypress trees covered in hanging moss stand beside shallow lakes.

In the past, people drained swamps to make dry land. They cut down the trees for lumber. Today, people know it is important to protect the plants and animals of the Great Dismal Swamp.

The Great Dismal Swamp is a place for ecotourists.

North Carolina has
many farms.

Visitors to the Great Dismal Swamp can hike and
ride bicycles on trails. They can canoe in the waters.
Photographers take pictures of the natural wonders.

In the spring, visitors come to watch the area's nesting
songbirds. Summer is not as popular. Muggy weather and
insects make the area unappealing to visitors.

The Farmlands

Beyond the marshlands, North Carolina's land slowly
changes to rich farmlands. This part of the Coastal Plain is
home to many of the state's agricultural products. The state's
leading product is tobacco. Other major crops are peanuts
and sweet potatoes.

Rich soil is one of North Carolina's greatest natural
resources. The central and western areas of the Coastal
Plain provide excellent farmland.

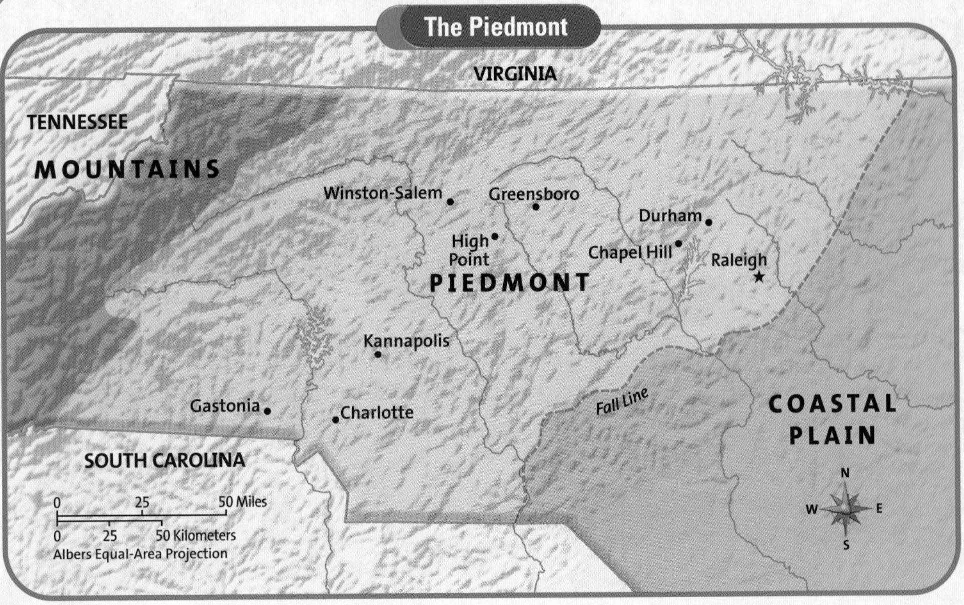

The Piedmont map showing:

VIRGINIA

TENNESSEE

MOUNTAINS

Winston-Salem, Greensboro

High Point, Chapel Hill, Durham, Raleigh ★

PIEDMONT

Kannapolis

Gastonia, Charlotte, Fall Line

COASTAL PLAIN

SOUTH CAROLINA

0   25   50 Miles
0   25   50 Kilometers
Albers Equal-Area Projection

N W E S

The Piedmont

The Piedmont area is in the center of the state. The French word *piedmont* means "foot of the mountain." This area is also known as the foothills, or hills near mountains.

The Fall Line

An area known as the fall line divides the Coastal Plain from the Piedmont. The fall line is an imaginary line that separates the lowlands from the hills. Rivers drop from the rocky hills into the flatter valleys. This area has many beautiful waterfalls.

Reed Gold Mine

The first gold was discovered in the Piedmont. In 1799, young Conrad Reed found a 17-pound yellow rock in a creek. They used it for a doorstop before they discovered its value!

Booming Cities and Human Resources

The Piedmont region has the largest number of people in the state. The state's capital, Raleigh, is here. So is Charlotte, the largest city in the state. The area provides jobs in manufacturing, research, and education.

Farming and Mineral Resources

The farms of the Piedmont raise many of the chickens eaten in the United States. Hogs, turkeys, and dairy cows are also raised in the area. The major crops of the Piedmont are wheat, soybeans, apples, and peaches.

Granite and shale are the major mineral resources of the Piedmont. Clay is also found in the Piedmont. American Indians in North Carolina have used clay to make pottery for hundreds of years.

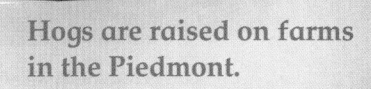

Hogs are raised on farms in the Piedmont.

Highboy in High Point

High Point, North Carolina, is home to the world's tallest highboy. The giant chest of drawers reaches 32 feet into the sky.

North Carolina's Economic Capital

Manufacturing

North Carolina is the number one producer of textiles, furniture, and tobacco products in the United States. The craftsmanship of the furniture made in the Piedmont city of Thomasville is well known.

The factories and machinery used to make these goods are valuable capital resources. The factory workers are valuable human resources.

Textiles are a major industry in North Carolina.

Industries

North Carolina is well known for medical and high-tech research. Many people have jobs in education and health care, as well. Service industries provide many jobs in North Carolina's booming cities.